Places in Our Community

Our Park

by Lisa J. Amstutz

PEBBLE
a capstone imprint

Pebble Plus is published by Pebble, a Capstone imprint.
1710 Roe Crest Drive, North Mankato, Minnesota 56003
www.capstonepub.com

Library of Congress Cataloging-in-Publication data is available on the Library of Congress website.
ISBN 978-1-9771-1262-0 (library binding)
ISBN 978-1-9771-1769-4 (paperback)
ISBN 978-1-9771-1268-2 (eBook PDF)

Summary: Parks are important places in our community. It takes many community helpers to keep a park clean
and beautiful. Readers will learn about who works at a park, what the workers do, and what makes a city park
special. Simple, at-level text and vibrant photos help readers learn all about community parks.

Editorial Credits
Editor: Mari Schuh; Designers: Kay Fraser and Ashlee Suker; Media Researcher: Eric Gohl;
Production Specialist: Katy LaVigne

Photo Credits
Alamy: Andrey Khokhlov, 19, imageBROKER, 9, ZUMA Press, Inc., 11; iStockphoto: FatCamera, 17, juefraphoto, 7;
Shutterstock: Adamov_d, 22, Africa Studio, cover, 5, Alexander Chelmodeev, 22–23, Alexxndr, 2 (notebooks),
Betelgejze, 3, karelnoppe, 24, Monkey Business Images, 1, Take Photo, back cover, 2 (playground), varuna, 4, 6, 8, 10,
12, 14, 16, 18, 20, Wang Sing, 21, wavebreakmedia, 13; SuperStock: Design Pics/Axiom Photographic/Paul Miles, 15

Note to Parents and Teachers

The Places in Our Community set supports national social studies standards related to people,
places, and environments. This book describes and illustrates a park and the people who work
there. The images support early readers in understanding the text. The repetition of words
and phrases helps early readers learn new words. This book also introduces early readers to
subject-specific vocabulary words, which are defined in the Glossary section. Early readers
may need assistance to read some words and to use the Table of Contents, Glossary, Read More,
Internet Sites, Critical Thinking Questions, and Index sections of the book.

All internet sites appearing in back matter were available and accurate when this book was sent to press.

Table of Contents

Let's Visit a Park!

Is there a park near your home? A park is a place to play. But taking care of a park can be hard work. Let's meet some park staff!

Who Works at Parks?

Look at the flowers! Landscapers make the park look pretty. They take care of the plants. They trim bushes and mow the lawn.

Please, follow the rules.
Security or police officers
help keep the park safe. They
patrol the park. They make sure
people follow park rules.

Want to go on a nature hike? Naturalists help park visitors learn about nature. They lead hikes. They teach people the names of plants and animals.

Join the group and have fun! Program directors plan group classes. People learn to dance and do yoga. These activities help people stay healthy.

Splash! Lifeguards watch swimmers closely. They rescue people who are in danger. Lifeguards also make sure people follow pool rules.

Swim teachers help kids learn to swim. Swim teachers might be lifeguards too. Knowing how to swim keeps people safe in the water.

Keeping Parks Clean

Please, don't litter!

Custodians keep the park clean.

They empty trash cans and

clean buildings. Visitors can

keep parks clean too.

A day at the park is fun!

You can hike or swim. You can

play basketball or baseball.

The choices are endless! What

is your favorite park activity?

Glossary

lifeguard—a person trained to help swimmers

naturalist—a person who studies and teaches about natural history

nature—everything in the world that isn't made by people

patrol—to protect and watch an area

rescue—to save someone who is in danger

rule—an instruction that tells people what to do; rules help people learn, stay healthy, and stay safe

staff—a group of people who work for the same company or school

yoga—exercises that help people be relaxed and fit

Read More

Evans, Shira. *Helpers in Your Neighborhood*. Washington, D.C.: National Geographic Kids, 2018.

Finn, Peter. *Go to the Park!* New York: Gareth Stevens Publishing, 2020.

Manley, Erika S. *Park Rangers*. Community Helpers. Minneapolis: Jump! Inc., 2020.

Internet Sites

People, Occupations, Jobs, and Community
https://www.enchantedlearning.com/themes/communityhelpers.shtml

PBS Kids: Swimming Lessons
https://pbskids.org/video/wild-kratts/2365751984

Community Club from Scholastic
http://teacher.scholastic.com/commclub/

Critical Thinking Questions

1. What does a landscaper do at a park?

2. Name two other people who work at parks.

3. How can people use parks to stay active and healthy?

Index